T,

Daimler
Buses in camera

Right: The revolutionary twin-engined KPL of 1910 (see page 9). / Daimler

Overleaf: The CH6 with its modern-looking deep radiator, in 1930 (see page 21). / Ian Allan Library

Daimler
Buses in camera

Stewart J. Brown MCIT

LONDON

IAN ALLAN LTD

First published 1978

ISBN 0 7110 0902 3

© Ian Allan Ltd 1978

Published by Ian Allan Ltd, Shepperton, Surrey;
and printed in the United Kingdom by
Ian Allan Printing Ltd

Contents

Acknowledgements

Thanks are due to all the people who responded so willingly to my call for photographs. The final selection was made from well over 1,000 views available to me. Many people provided help in other ways and among these are Gavin Booth, D. R. Howard, G. R. Mills, T. W. Moore, J. R. Neale, G. J. Travers, Andrew Whyte and his colleagues at Daimler-Jaguar, and the staff of Coventry Museums department. The PSV Circle kindly gave permission to extract information from its records.

Left: *A CVD6 coach of Highland Omnibuses seen in Inverness (see page 50).*
/ Stewart J. Brown

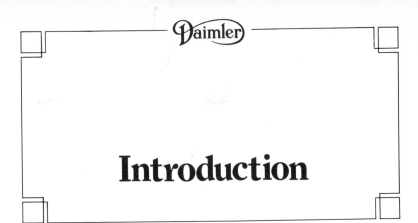

Introduction

This book does not purport to be a history of Daimler bus production, but is rather an album of photographs showing the development of Daimler buses. However, having said that, a little bit of history is not inappropriate . . .

Gottlieb Daimler was born in 1834 and in 1882 set up his first research workshop in Cannstatt, Germany. An English engineer, Frederick Richard Simms, met Daimler in Bremen at the end of the 1880s and subsequently acquired the exclusive Daimler engine patent rights for the United Kingdom.

In 1893 Simms formed the Daimler Motor Syndicate Ltd, operating from a railway arch at Putney Bridge, London. The year 1896 saw the formation of the Daimler Motor Co Ltd and a move to Coventry, the town with which the Daimler name will always be linked.

Although Daimler is best known as a manufacturer of quality cars, commercial vehicles have been built since the company's earliest days. A double-deck bus was exhibited at Olympia in 1908. This petrol-electric vehicle had a radiator with a fluted top tank, a feature introduced on cars in 1904 and now recognised as Daimler's trade mark. However, most early buses had the word 'Daimler' cast in the top tank; the fluted radiator was not usually fitted to buses until 1929 when it appeared on the CF6 model. Proof of early activity was an order in 1912 from the Tramways (MET) Omnibus Co Ltd for 350 Daimler double-deckers — a sizeable order by any standards — for operation in London. By this time Daimler had been acquired by the Birmingham Small Arms Co Ltd and renamed the Daimler Company Ltd.

In 1912 Daimler's first link with the Associated Equipment Company was formed when Daimler was appointed sales agents for any AEC chassis built surplus to the requirements of the London General Omnibus Company, at that time owners of AEC. Co-operation with AEC reached its peak in 1926 when a joint company was formed. This was the Associated Daimler Company — ADC — but it was short lived and the participants went their separate ways in 1929 although AEC diesel engines were installed as an option in Daimler chassis from 1934 until the late 1940s.

The 1930s saw the diesel engine gain universal acceptance in bus chassis and Daimler adopted the Gardner 5LW and 6LW as its standard engines in the second half of the decade. These were coupled to Daimler's preselective gearbox and fluid flywheel which had been announced in 1930 and which undoubtedly did much for Daimler's popularity with urban bus operators.

Transport Vehicles (Daimler) Ltd was formed in 1936 to manufacture bus and coach chassis; car manufacture stayed with the Daimler Company Ltd. In the same year trolleybus production commenced and 25 were built before the war started in 1939. Production continued in the 1949-1951 period but only 92 postwar trolleybus chassis were built.

Left: *An Aberdeen Corporation CVG6 on a city tour passes the 120ft high Girdleness lighthouse which can be seen for 19 miles. The bus was new in 1964 and was one of the penultimate batch of this model delivered to Aberdeen. It had a 66-seat Alexander body.* / Stewart J. Brown

Normal bus production ceased in 1940 (the Daimler works were badly damaged in the November 1940 air raid on Coventry) but in 1942 the Ministry of War Transport announced the resumption of bus production by Daimler and 100 Wolverhampton-built CWG5s were delivered to operators in 1943. Further chassis followed, initially with AEC engines but from 1944 including some with Daimler's own diesel engine, the CD6, which had been under development in 1939.

The postwar Victory series chassis appeared in 1946 and continued in production — much modified — until 1971. In the meantime the underfloor-engined Freeline (the first Daimler bus to have a model name) had come and gone; and the rear-engined Fleetline — destined to be the last bus to bear the Daimler name — had appeared in 1960. This was also the year in which the company was taken over by Jaguar Cars Ltd. A rear-engined single-decker chassis was unveiled in 1962 and this was developed into the Roadliner which was produced from 1965 to 1972.

In 1966 another name change took place (to Daimler Transport Vehicles Ltd) and in April 1968 the company finally became part of the Leyland empire.

Over the years Daimler buses have found ready buyers in many overseas countries. There were Daimlers in New York in 1910; more recent markets have included Australia, Canada, Hong Kong, Portugal and South Africa.

The largest fleet of Daimlers is operated by London Transport which has 2,646 Fleetlines in service or on order. However Leyland is now bringing the Daimler bus story to an end. Current Fleetlines are referred to by their maker as Leylands and carry Leyland badges. It is Leyland's intention to phase out the Fleetline in 1979 as production of the new Leyland Titan TN15 gets under way.

Which makes this a fitting time to recall the story of the Daimler bus.

Colchester   *Stewart J. Brown*

Below: *A CRG6LX-33 with 80-seat Park Royal body seen in Johannesburg (see page 92).* / Stewart J. Brown

Early Days

At Olympia in March 1908 Daimler exhibited a purpose-built bus — a petrol-electric double-decker for the Gearless Motor Omnibus Company Ltd of London. The next model was the advanced KPL, built in 1910. The petrol-electric KPL was of all-steel chassis-less construction — probably the first bus to use this type of construction — and was unusual in that it had *two* 12hp engines. One engine was mounted on each side and drove each rear wheel. Four-wheel brakes were another advanced feature. The KPL initials stood for Knight (engine), Pieper (transmission) and Lanchester (worm drive).

From this period until 1931 all Daimler buses had sleeve-valve petrol engines, usually of a four-cylinder design. Early Daimler purchasers included Birmingham, Chesterfield, Manchester, Rotherham, Sheffield and Vienna. In London, British Automobile Traction Co and the Gearless Motor Omnibus Co purchased Daimlers and it was from a London operator that

Below: Daimler's 1908 petrol-electric double-decker featured the fluted radiator top tank which later became a Daimler trademark. On the left is the revolutionary twin-engined KPL of 1910. The driving position was far forward for the time; most contemporary buses had a long bonnet in front of the driver. / Daimler

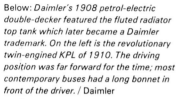

Daimler received its first large order — 350 double-deckers for the Tramways (MET) Omnibus Co. These appeared in 1912 and bore a strong resemblance to the London General Omnibus Company's famous B type. This was hardly surprising since Daimler had secured the services of Frank Searle, previously the LGOC's chief engineer.

The CB, CC and CD models were produced in the period immediately before the 1914-1918 war and many of the Daimler chassis produced for military use were converted for use as buses after the war. In 1919 the CK was introduced but differed little from pre-war models. It had a 5.1 litre four-cylinder engine which was also installed in the 1925 CL and CM single-deck models. The short-wheelbase CK was suitable for double-deck or single-deck bodywork.

In 1920, after experimenting with pneumatic tyres the previous year, Daimler offered them as an option to solid tyres on certain models.

June 1926 saw the formation of the Associated Daimler Company, owned jointly by Daimler and AEC. This was not the first association between the companies. In 1912 Daimler had been appointed sales agents for any AEC chassis produced surplus to the requirements of the London General Omnibus Company which at that time owned AEC. Some early AEC chassis had been fitted with Daimler engines and when the Daimler factory was unable to cope with demand for its products some orders were built at AEC's works in Walthamstow.

The Associated Daimler Company, generally known as ADC, initially used AEC chassis designs with AEC or Daimler engines. The former were normally four-cylinder 5.1 litre poppet valve types; the latter six-cylinder 3.57 litre sleeve-valve. The first single-deckers were the 416 (forward control) and 417 (normal control) models which had a suffix letter A or D to indicate whether an AEC or a Daimler engine was fitted. The contemporary 415 was a smaller single-decker and the 409 was a double-decker derived from the AEC NS type and later developed to become the 422. ADC's other double-decker was the three-axle 802. AEC trolleybuses were also sold under the ADC banner.

In October 1927 the Daimler-engined 423 (normal control) and 424 (forward control) were introduced, followed by the AEC-engined 426 (forward control) and 427 (normal control) which replaced the 416 and 417. These were built at their respective engine maker's factories. The 425 was a modified 426 supplied only to United Automobile Services.

Below: *The Tramways (MET) Omnibus Co ordered 350 double-deckers from Daimler. This view shows one in use for driver training.* / Ian Allan Library

Above: *The KPL was later rebuilt with a covered top deck. The extra weight of the cover would have made this tilt test of more than usual interest in a period when double-deck buses were invariably open-toppers.* / Daimler

Left: *This view shows that the upper deck side windows were unglazed. Canvas screens provided protection from the weather. This is believed to be the only KPL to have been built.* / Daimler

Left: *Early export deliveries included this double-decker for New York. It retained right-hand drive but the open staircase did, of course, ascend from the right side of the bus rather than from the left as in Britain.* / Daimler

Right: *A single-decker of the same period in the Colwills fleet, which was associated with Crosville. Colwills also operated Daimler charabancs.* / R. L. Wilson collection

Below right: *Bournemouth bought a pair of Brush-bodied Daimlers in 1914. They were short-lived however, the chassis being requisitioned by the War Department in that same year.* / Daimler

Below: *A pair of CC models of Sheffield Corporation Tramways. They were new in 1913.* / Daimler

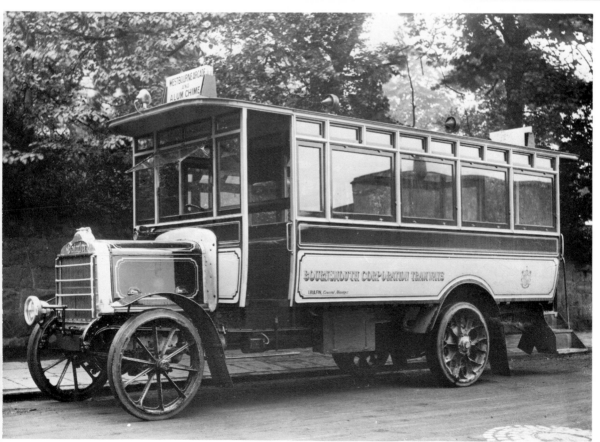

Above left: *A 1912 CC in the Halifax fleet. A*
***windscreen** is fitted to provide a little*
protection** for the driver. The weight **written
on the side panels is divided between front
wheels and hind wheels. / Daimler

Left: *The Worcester Electric Traction Co, **part***
*of the BET group, operated this charabanc **of***
the 1910s. / Daimler

Above: *There were some advances in*
charabanc design as illustrated by this
specimen from the following decade. The
most obvious change is the fitment of
pneumatic tyres and headlights of more
modern outline. But the body is smoother in
outline and the scuttle is neater too.
/ Daimler

Right: *In 1922 Potteries Electric Traction*
(which became Potteries Motor Traction in
*1933) purchased this Daimler Y with **29-seat***
Brush body. The chassis was reconditioned
*ex-War Department, and was built **during the***
1914-18 war. It was withdrawn in 1930.
/ Ian Allan Library

Below: *This ADC 416A was new to the Glasgow General Omnibus Co in 1928. The 30-seat body was by Metcalfe.* / R. L. Grieves collection

Bottom: *Of more modern appearance was the ADC 424, as illustrated by this Crosville example, also new in 1928. This had a Daimler engine and was a forerunner of the CF6.* / R. L. Wilson collection

Through the Thirties

With the ending of ADC in 1929, Daimler continued production of the 423 and 424 models which had been made at Coventry. The plain ADC radiator was given a fluted top tank as used on Daimler cars. The CF6 model was developed in 1929 when a 5.76 litre six-cylinder sleeve valve engine was fitted to the 423 and 424 chassis. This engine had been fitted to some of the ADC 802 six-wheelers and had also been installed in Guy chassis. The CF6 was produced during 1929 and 1930, when it was replaced by the CG6 which used the CF6 engine and transmission in a new low frame chassis. Normal control chassis were dropped from the Daimler range with the demise of the CF6.

The CG6 with its low frame and modern deep radiator set the style for Daimler buses of the 1930s, although it was only in production for about a year. The main reason for its short life was Daimler's adoption of the preselector gearbox and fluid flywheel. This enabled the driver to select a gear before actually making a gear change; the gear he selected was only engaged when he pressed the gear engaging pedal which took the place of the clutch used with a normal gearbox. It was easier to use than a conventional gearbox and clutch too, and in October 1930 it made its appearance in the CH6 model which was demonstrated in various parts of Britain.

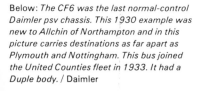

Below: *The CF6 was the last normal-control Daimler psv chassis. This 1930 example was new to Allchin of Northampton and in this picture carries destinations as far apart as Plymouth and Nottingham. This bus joined the United Counties fleet in 1933. It had a Duple body. / Daimler*

The CH6 had inherited the sleeve valve engine of the CG6 but operators were by that time looking for a normal poppet valve engine — hence the appearance of the CP6 (P for poppet), announced at the end of 1931. The engine for the CP6 was developed from the sleeve-valve engine and had a capacity of 6.56 litres.

By this time the diesel engine had appeared and was quickly gaining acceptance as a practical and economical power unit for buses. Daimler did not produce a diesel engine and so turned to Gardner which had introduced its LW range of diesels in 1931. Initially the 5LW, a five-cylinder 7 litre unit, was chosen and the resultant model called the COG5 (**C**ommercial, **O**il, **G**ardner, 5 cylinder). The first were running in 1933 and production commenced officially in 1934. The combination of Gardner engine and preselector gearbox soon became popular, particularly with municipal operators. Although a four-speed gearbox was standard, a five-speed version was offered as an option.

From 1934 single-deck and double-deck chassis were differentiated by an SD or DD suffix after the chassis designation — for example COG5DD.

A logical companion for the COG5 was the COG6, which appeared in 1935. It featured the six-cylinder Gardner 6LW engine of 8.4 litres capacity. The 6LW developed 102bhp against the 5LW output of 85bhp and catered for operators who required more power. It had a longer bonnet and was offered on the home market as a double-decker only. Both the COG5 and COG6 continued in production until 1940. Production of the petrol-engined CP6 ceased in the middle of the decade.

Below: A 1929 CF6 of the Belfast Omnibus Co. The CF6 used a sleeve-valve engine and was the last model to have a short radiator. The advert in the background for the Central Furnishing Co offers customers a refund of their bus fare — if they spend £15 or more! / R. C. Ludgate collection

Although Gardner was the principal supplier of oil engines for Daimler buses, it was not the only one. Between 1934 and 1940 Coventry Corporation specified AEC engines. The 7.7 litre version was fitted to all COA6s except for three which had the larger 8.8 litre unit. Only COA6DD models were built and although the model was available to all operators Coventry was the only buyer.

The COS4 is a less well known Daimler variant. Ten of these were supplied to Newcastle Corporation in 1935 and had Armstrong Saurer four-cylinder engines. This followed an experiment by Newcastle in which a six-cylinder Armstrong Saurer diesel engine had been installed in a CP6 chassis. A unique COT4, with four-cylinder Tangye oil engine joined the Edinburgh Corporation fleet in 1934; it was converted to COG5 specification two years later.

There were variants on the COG5 and COG6 theme. The single-deck COG5/40 introduced in 1936 had a vertical, instead of a sloping, radiator and a more compact engine installation. This was designed to allow another row of seats to be fitted within an overall length of 27ft 6in — then the legal maximum in Britain. The 40 referred to its theoretical maximum seating capacity. A double-deck equivalent, the COG5/60, was produced in 1939 for Coventry.

The COG6/40 was an export single-deck chassis with an 18ft 9in wheelbase which compared with 17ft 6in for the home market COG5SD.

Three-axle six-wheel COG5s were built for use in China in 1940 but were sunk in transit. A three-axle COG6 for Leicester was destroyed in an air raid in Coventry in 1940.

Below: *A CF6 chassis formed the basis of this luxurious coach supplied to Glenton Friars for use on the London to Newcastle service and seen here before delivery. There is no immediately obvious explanation for the two men sitting in the roof luggage carrier.* / Daimler

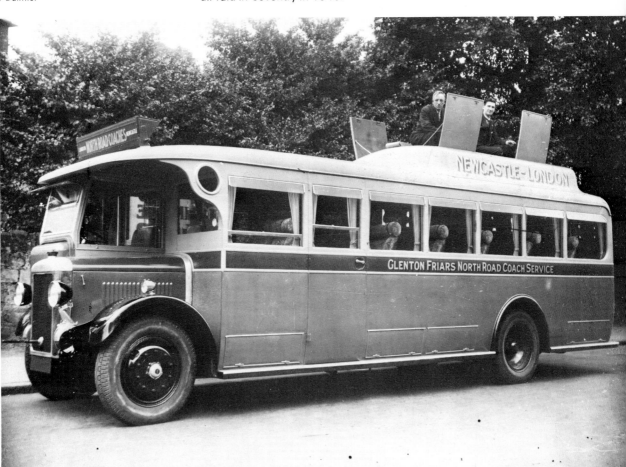

Left: *Two 1930* Modern Transport *road test vehicles illustrate developments in that year. The CF6, unusual in having double-deck bodywork, was tested in June. This demonstrator, in a commendably simple livery for that time, had front entrance, rear exit bodywork. The* Modern Transport *tester recorded a top speed of 47mph.*
/ Ian Allan Library

Below: *Only four months later, in October 1930,* Modern Transport *tried the CH6 with its new preselector gearbox and modern-looking deep radiator — behind which there still lurked a sleeve-valve petrol engine. The deep radiator first appeared on the manual gearbox CG6 and was used on the CP6 (poppet-valve) model which followed the CH6. This bus had a Park Royal body.*
/ Ian Allan Library

Above left: *The CG6, CH6 and CP6 were of more modern appearance with a deeper radiator. This CH6 was delivered to Edinburgh Corporation in 1930 and was an early specimen of a Daimler with preselector gearbox. It had a 29-seat Hume body. A Gardner 5LW oil engine replaced the original Daimler petrol unit in 1935 and the bus was withdrawn in 1939.* / Gavin Booth collection

Left: *This 1929 CF6 is seen when new in the ownership of Thomson's Tours, Edinburgh. In 1930 it was taken over by SMT. In this photograph, taken in Princes Street, it is loaded ready for a run to London — note the passengers' luggage on the roof. Thomson's offered Rolls-Royce cars for hire, as well as running an Edinburgh to London sightseeing service, according to the board on the building. The four-legged ghost in front of the radiator is someone who moved during the comparatively long exposure.* / Daimler

Above: *Stockton Corporation owned this CH6 with Park Royal body. It was new in 1930.* / Daimler

Right: *This 1932 CP6 of Wallasey Corporation Motors had 48-seat two-door English Electric bodywork. It was sold to Kingston-upon-Hull Corporation in 1941. Wallasey also ran CF6 double-deckers.* / R. L. Wilson collection

Above: *This batch of twenty COG5 with Weymann bodywork were the first buses in the Hull fleet to feature the streamlined livery which was to be a feature of the city for 40 years. New in 1936, this bus was destroyed in 1941.* / Daimler

Left: *City Tramways of Cape Town received COG6 models with Weymann bodywork similar to that on the Hull COG5. Note the spelling differences between the Afrikaans and English language advertisements and the deep slatted sun shades over the windows. Other South African cities to operate Daimlers included Durban, Johannesburg and Kimberley.* / Daimler

Above: *New Zealand was another early export market. The North Shore Transport Co used this as a one-man-operated bus.* / Daimler

Left: *A fleet of 35 COG5/40 was purchased by Birmingham City Transport in 1935. This one had a Strachan body and joined the fleet of Stevenson, Spath in 1951. It was scrapped ten years later.* / Roy Marshall

Below left: *This 1935 COG5 ran for Birmingham City Transport until 1954 when it was converted to a snow-plough. It had 54-seat Metro-Cammell bodywork and was one of 800 broadly similar buses.* / Roy Marshall

Right: *This is one of a pair of COG5 with 48-seat metal framed English Electric bodywork which joined the Lancaster fleet in 1936. It survived until 1952.* / Roy Marshall

Above right: *With the double-deckers Lancaster also received two COG5/40 single-deckers. They had English Electric rear-entrance bodies with 39-seats — only nine fewer than in the double-deckers. Note the upright radiator of the COG5/40, compared with the sloping radiator of the double-decker* / R. L. Wilson

Above: *The standard Edinburgh single-decker from 1936 to 1938 was the COG5. This was one of ten Weymann-bodied examples delivered in 1937; it was withdrawn in 1953.* / Roy Marshall

Above left: *Wolverhampton purchased six Park Royal-bodied COG5 in 1936. All were sold in 1944, three going to Caerphilly and three to West Bromwich where this one is seen in 1959. It was withdrawn the following year.* / T. W. Moore

Left: *Glasgow purchased its first Daimlers in 1937 — a batch of 25 Weymann-bodied COG6. All were sold in 1951; this one is seen crossing the Clyde on Victoria Bridge shortly before its withdrawal.* / R. L. Grieves collection

Centre right: *After having standardised on Thornycrofts since 1925, the Stalybridge, Hyde, Mossley & Dukinfield Transport & Electricity Board turned to Daimlers in 1937. This 38-seat Northern Counties-bodied COG5/40 was one of eight purchased in that year. All were withdrawn between 1956 and 1960. Sharp eyesight would be needed to read the route number.* / R. L. Wilson

Bottom right: *For double-deckers SHMD usually favoured the COG6. This one, also with Northern Counties body, was new in 1939 and gave 19 years' service. It formed part of a batch of ten.* / Roy Marshall

Left: From 1937 to 1939 Derby bought Brush-bodied COG5. This is one of ten delivered in 1938 and it ran as a bus until 1957, when it was converted to a tower wagon. / Roy Marshall

Right: Aberdare bought 24 COG5 double- and single-deckers between 1934 and 1938. This was one of the last, a Willowbrook 38-seat COG5/40 of 1938. It had a rear entrance and was sold in 1956. / Roy Marshall

Below right: This Dundee COG5 with locally-built Dickson body entered service in 1940 and was one of eight similar buses (plus eight with Weymann bodies). All were sold in 1956/7. Before the introduction of exterior advertising Dundee buses carried the city's name on the between decks panelling. / Roy Marshall

Below: Forward entrance Weymann bodywork was fitted to six South Shields COG5. This 56-seater was one of three purchased in 1938. It was photographed in 1950, and remained in service until 1957. / Roy Marshall

Left: *A 1939 Metro-Cammell-bodied COG6 which ran for West Bromwich Corporation for 24 years. It was one of 31.* / Roy Marshall

Right: *Twelve Weymann-bodied COG5 joined the Trent fleet in 1939. The forward-entrance body still looked pleasantly modern in this 1948 view. This bus was withdrawn in 1954.* / Roy Marshall

Below right: *Gash of Newark, which purchased many Daimlers in the late 1940s, operated this 1939 COG5/40 on its Newark to Nottingham via the villages service. It had Willowbrook 39-seat bodywork and was one of a pair. It was withdrawn in 1954.* / Roy Marshall

Below: *West Hartlepool Corporation purchased a pair of Roe-bodied COG5 in 1939. The fully-fronted bodywork was presumably designed to allow the diesel bus to blend in with the undertaking's trolleybuses. Both buses were sold in 1956 to Trimdon Motor Services, the north-eastern independent.* / Roy Marshall

Above: *This COG5 of the West Monmouthshire Omnibus Board had been destined for an operator in Southern Rhodesia when it was diverted to South Wales in 1941. It had a Weymann body 8ft wide and 30ft long and was one of the first two-axle motor buses of these dimensions to run in Britain. The Daimler lettering on the radiator was a standard feature of export buses. It was fitted with an AEC engine in 1956 and sold four years later. Seven similar buses were delivered to PMT. / Roy Marshall*

Right: *Five 8ft wide Metro-Cammell-bodied COG6 built for Johannesburg Municipal Transport entered service with British operators in 1941/2. One went to West Mon, where it joined the Southern Rhodesian COG5, and four were delivered to Birmingham City Transport including the one shown here. / Don Morris*

War and Victory

Production of pre-war chassis ceased in 1940 and the Daimler factory was badly damaged in the November 1940 air raids. In 1942 it was announced that Daimler double-deck chassis would be available again — produced in Wolverhampton. The first models to appear were 100 CWG5, a modified COG5, which entered service in 1943. These were followed in September of the same year by the CWA6, which had the AEC 7.7 litre engine, and was similar to the last COA6 models built for Coventry. The W in the chassis designation indicated **W**artime.

Before the outbreak of war Daimler had been developing its own diesel engine. This was the CD6, a six-cylinder 8.6 litre unit and in 1944 the first of these were installed in CWD6 chassis. A CWG6 model was exported in small numbers. In all about 1,400 wartime Daimler chassis were built and most were fitted with bodies to Ministry of Supply specification — now better known as utility bodywork. The MoS specification body had five bays; was of wooden framed construction; had only one opening window on each side of each deck; one (front) destination screen; and, from 1943,

Below: *The CWA6 was the most numerous wartime variant. Those supplied to Aberdeen Corporation had a long life — this one lasted until 1965. It is seen in the later years of its life by which time its utility Duple body had been rebuilt by its owner. It was new in 1943.* / Stewart J. Brown

wooden slatted seats. Wartime bodies on Daimler chassis were built by Brush, Duple, Massey, Northern Countries, Park Royal, Roe and Weymann.

After the war came the **V**ictory range — the CVA6, CVD6, and CVG5. These appeared in 1946 — and were soon joined by the CVG6 — and were developments of the wartime models. All had a wheelbase of 17ft 2½in and a preselector gearbox. The most popular models were those powered by the Gardner 6LW or the Daimler CD6 engines; the latter was frequently chosen by coach operators. The last AEC-engined CVA6 entered service in 1950.

The CD650 was announced in 1948. This double-decker was based on the CVD6 but had a 10.6 litre Daimler engine, power-assisted steering (for the first time on a British bus), and power-assisted brakes. Externally it could be distinguished by its wide radiator. An export single-decker — the CD650SD was offered with a 20ft wheelbase. Only fourteen CD650s entered service in Britain; about 50, mostly single-deckers, were exported.

A special model was built in 1949 for operation in Cape Town. This was the CVG6/6 which had a Gardner 6LW engine installed in a six-wheel, three-axle chassis fitted with 30ft long Weymann bodywork. The chassis was related to Daimler's six-wheel trolleybus chassis and had the wide CD650 style radiator. Twenty were built.

Below: *Northern Counties wartime bodywork had a tall gaunt appearance. This 1944 CWA6 is seen in service with Bradford Corporation in 1949. Uniformless conductors are obviously not a new phenomenon.* / Roy Marshall

Above left: Chester Corporation received a number of wartime Daimlers including this 1944 CWA6 with Brush bodywork, photographed in the city centre in 1954. / Roy Marshall

Left: Lowbridge Brush bodywork was fitted to this 1944 CWA6 of South Yorkshire, the Pontefract based independent. / G. R. Mills

Below: The drabness of wartime buses is illustrated by this 1945 CWA6 of Trent. It has a lowbridge Duple body and was withdrawn in 1956. / Roy Marshall

Left: *This Newcastle Corporation CWA6 was new in 1945 and had Massey bodywork. / Don Morris*

Below: *Sutherland of Peterhead received a pair of Massey-bodied CWA6 in 1946, by which time less utilitarian bodywork was being built. Sutherland had authority from the Regional Transport Commissioners to have platform doors fitted to utility buses. The Sutherland fleet was taken over by W. Alexander & Sons Ltd in 1950 and by 1964 this CWA6 was in the livery of Alexander's (Midland). / Stewart J. Brown*

Above: *In 1946 Dundee Corporation purchased a trio of CWD6 with Duple bodies of angular but attractive appearance. This view shows the second of the batch in Dundee's 1950s green and cream livery; the three buses served the city until 1966.* / Real Photographs

Left: *This 1946 CVD6 had a typical Roe highbridge body of the period with the patented straight staircase and unequal depth windows on each deck. It was one of two supplied to Blair & Palmer of Carlisle but when photographed in Saltcoats in August 1961 had joined the fleet of AA Motor Services. The AA name came from the initials of the terminal towns of the trunk route between Ayr and Ardrossan.* / R. L. Wilson

Below: *Reliance of York owned this 1947 CVG5, an unusual choice for an independent. The coach-like Barnaby body had 35 bus seats.* / G. R. Mills

Bottom: *In 1947/48 the MTT, Adelaide, purchased CVG6s with Commonwealth Engineering 54-seat double-deck bodies of a basically pre-war design. The cab windows were very small by contemporary British standards and the rear-hinged cab door was unusual. It was photographed in 1961.* / N. Mackintosh

Above: *A fleet of Daimlers visited Copenhagen in 1948 on a sales drive. Nearest the camera is a Glasgow 1946 CWD6 with Brush body. Alongside is a Metro-Cammell-bodied CVD6 of Birmingham and then Brush-bodied CVD6 of Bradford, the SHMD Joint Board and Nottingham. The last bus is a CVG6 with Metro-Cammell body from the Salford fleet.* / R. L. Grieves collection

Left: *The CVA6 was a comparatively rare model. This one, with even rarer Welsh Metal Industries lowbridge body, was new in 1948 to Yeoman's Motors of Canon Pyon. Platform doors were still uncommon when this bus was built.* / R. L. Wilson

Left: *Cleethorpes Corporation purchased three Willowbrook bodied CVD6 in 1948. The Cleethorpes municipal bus fleet was amalgamated with neighbouring Grimsby in 1957.* / Don Morris

Right: *Seen when new and prior to painting in City Tramways' livery, this is one of 20 Weymann-bodied CVG6/6 delivered to the Cape Town operator in 1949. These 30ft long buses had CD650 style wide radiators.* / Ian Allan Library

Below right: *An East Lancs-bodied CVD6 of the Stalybridge, Hyde, Mossley and Dukinfield undertaking seen in Princes Street, Stockport in April 1961. It was one of ten delivered in 1949 and was withdrawn in 1968.* / A. Moyes

Below: *Between 1947 and 1949 the Alexander fleet acquired a number of Burlingham-bodied CVD6 coaches. When the company split into three units in 1961 most of the Daimlers passed to Alexander's (Midland). One of four to join Alexander's (Northern) is shown in Stonehaven in its new cream and yellow livery. It was new in March 1948.* / Stewart J. Brown

Above left: *Colchester Corporation ordered ten of these Roberts-bodied CVD6. Five were delivered in the spring of 1949 but the remainder were diverted to Brown of Markfield (one) and Accrington Corporation (four). These were the only Daimlers ever owned by Colchester and this one is shown in Head Street in the town centre in September 1961.* / G. R. Mills

Left: *W. Gash & Sons Ltd of Newark was the last British operator of exposed radiator Daimler double-deckers. This CVD6 was one of four with Strachan lowbridge bodies delivered in 1948 and later rebodied by Massey.* / G. R. Mills

Above: *After rebodying the 1948 CVD6s looked like this. The highbridge Massey body was built in 1958. The bus is seen on a school trip in Newark in March 1977.* / T. W. Moore

Right: *This Roberts-bodied CVD6 joined the Gash fleet in 1949 and was the sole survivor of a pair when photograhed being prepared for service in 1977.* / T. W. Moore

Left: *A traditional style of fleetname still embellished this 27-year old CVD6 in 1977. It had a Duple lowbridge body and was one of two intended for Skills of Nottingham but diverted to Gash.* / T. W. Moore

Right: *This 1950 CVD6 with Duple lowbridge body was one of three for Skill's of Nottingham — but the other two were diverted to Gash of Newark. The decorative trim on the side panels was a feature of contemporary Duple bodies.* / Daimler

Below right: *A less famous member of the Gash fleet was this CVD6 with Burlingham coach body. It was new in 1950.* / G. R. Mills

Below: *Kumasi Town Council in the Gold Coast (now Ghana) purchased many Daimlers in the late 1940s. Most had single-deck bodywork by Kumasi or Saunders-Roe but this one, new in 1949, had utilitarian Kumasi-built double-deck bodywork which made extensive use of mahogany. The windows were mostly unglazed and the staircase must have been incredibly narrow, judging by the small space blanked off in the rear corner.* / Daimler

Left: *In 1950 Burwell & District purchased this CVD6 with 56-seat Massey bodywork. It is seen in Burwell in November 1965. / G. R. Mills*

Below left: *The Longueville Motor Bus Co of Sydney bought CVG6 chassis to which were fitted fully fronted bodywork by Syd Wood. This one photograhed at McMahons Point in 1971 was new in 1950. / John A. Ward*

Right: *Salford City Transport built up a large fleet of CVG6 with Metro-Cammell bodies. This one was new in 1950 and is seen near Old Trafford 18 years later. A Salford City Transport badge was carried on the top of the radiator which had a shortened shell to minimise accident damage. / T. W. Moore*

Below: *One of 20 CVD6 with 56-seat Brush bodywork delivered to Derby Corporation in 1950 and photographed in the town centre in October 1964. / T. W. Moore*

Above: *A small number of CV-series chassis found use as non-psvs. One of the most flamboyant bodies was this one by Wilsdon of Solihull which housed a mobile printing room for the Birmingham Post & Mail.* / T. W. Moore

Left: *Glasgow Corporation buses rarely saw rural surroundings. This 1951 CVD6 is seen nearing Carmunnock, a village to the south of the city, which was served until 1941 by an independent operator. It was one of 39 similar buses with 56-seat Alexander bodies and is seen in 1964.* / Stewart J. Brown

Above right: *With the 39 CVD6 came one CD650, also bodied by Alexander. The extra width of the radiator on this more powerful bus is immediately apparent. Glasgow Corporation scrapped the chassis in 1960 and transferred the body to a CVD6.* / S. N. J. White

Right: *Aberdeen Corporation, Britain's most northerly municipal bus operator, purchased ten CVG6 with Brockhouse bodies in 1951. This one, photographed in 1964, was sold in 1966.* / Stewart J. Brown

Left: *Only 14 of the CD650 model were purchased by British operators. This one, new in 1951, had Willowbrook bodywork and was one of four which belonged to Blue Bus Services of Willington.* / T. W. Moore

Right: *The specification of this bus — rear entrance single-deck body — was somewhat old fashioned by the standards of 1952. It is a CVG5 of West Bromwich Corporation. A 1948 CVG6 follows; both buses have Metro-Cammell bodywork. Note the semaphore indicator arm still in use when the photograph was taken in 1964.* / T. W. Moore

Below right: *This CVG6 was one of 20 delivered to West Bromwich in 1952. Most of the batch survived to be acquired by the West Midlands Passenger Transport Executive in 1969 and the last examples were withdrawn in 1973. In this 1970 view the new West Midlands fleetname has been superimposed on the traditional West Bromwich livery.* / G. R. Mills

Below: *In June 1951 Alexander's of Falkirk put 13 unique CVD6 coaches into service. They had 37-seat Eastern Coach Works bodies of a type normally found only on Bristol chassis. This, the last one, saw further service with Highland Omnibuses from 1965 to 1967, in whose livery it is shown in Inverness.* / Stewart J. Brown

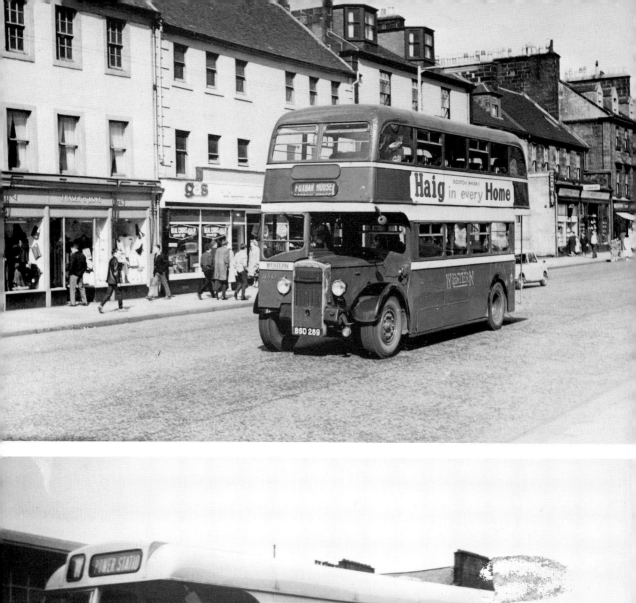

Left: *Western SMT received 18 Alexander-bodied CVG6 in 1951. The first one is seen in Paisley in 1965, its last year in service.* / Stewart J. Brown

Below left: *This is one of a trio of Northern Counties-bodied CVG5 buses delivered to Lancaster City Transport in 1952. Rebuilt to forward entrance and converted to permit one-man operation it was still running 25 years later.* / Don Morris

Right: *This 1952 CVG6 is one of a batch of 100 Daimlers delivered to Belfast Corporation. These were the last home market exposed radiator Daimlers and had 56-seat locally built Harkness bodies. Two of the batch were CVD6 models.* / R. C. Ludgate

Below: *Twenty CVG6 delivered to the Department of Government Transport in Sydney in 1952/53 were unusual in that they had the wide CD650 style radiator. The 31-seat two-door bodywork was by Commonwealth Engineering. All were withdrawn by 1973; this 1971 view shows one in Clifton Gardens, a Sydney suburb.* / John A. Ward

Right: *This CD650 chassis was built as a demonstration unit in 1948. It was sold to Tumilty of Irvine, a member of AA Motor Services, and fitted with a 57-seat Northern Counties body in 1954.* / Stewart J. Brown

Below: *One of the last CVD6 chassis to be used as the basis of a luxury coach was this Heaver-bodied example which was delivered to Burwell & District in 1954. The full-width cab disguised the then unfashionable exposed radiator.* / G. R. Mills

New look for the Fifties

Birmingham City Transport's new look tin front and bonnet, which hid the radiator and modernised the frontal appearance of its buses, was first fitted to CVD6s for that operator in 1951. It was soon offered as an alternative to the standard Daimler radiator and the last exposed radiator Daimlers for the home market were delivered to Belfast in 1953.

In 1951 Daimler revealed its first underfloor-engined single-decker which was also its first named bus chassis — the Freeline. Two versions of this heavyweight model were available: the D650HS and the G6HS (H for **H**orizontal engine). These used, respectively, a horizontal version of the 10.6 litre Daimler CD650 engine or the 8.4 litre Gardner 6HLW, the horizontal equivalent of the 6LW. The wheelbase was 16ft 4in (home) or 17ft 6in (export); a 20ft 4in model was soon added. The Freeline continued in production until 1964 by which time some 650 had been built. The last were delivered to Great Yarmouth Corporation.

Below: Daimler's original 'new look' front was of a design first used by Birmingham City Transport for all its double-deck bus deliveries, regardless of manufacturer. This 1953 Crossley-bodied CVG6 of that operator illustrates the attractive lines of the standard Daimler front of the period. This bus survived until 1975, by which time Birmingham City Transport had been absorbed by the West Midlands Passenger Transport Executive. / T. W. Moore

The majority of Freelines were exported (New Zealand and South Africa were the main markets) and less than 100 were sold in Britain. A G5HS model was listed with the Gardner 5HLW engine, but the only customer for this version was Bombay.

The CLG5 (L for Lightweight) was exhibited at the Earls Court Commercial Motor Show in 1952, had a Birmingham front, and was 10cwt lighter than a CVG6. The complete bus weighed only 6tons 2cwt and was the lightest double-decker on show. A range of CLG5, CLG6 and CLD6 double-deckers was proposed but was soon dropped and some of its weight-saving features incorporated on the standard CV range.

The Construction and Use Reguations were amended in 1956 to allow the operation of 30ft long two-axle double-deckers. Daimler produced a lengthened version of its CVG6 (by then the best-selling model) which was called the CVG6-30. This had an 18ft 6in wheelbase instead of 16ft 4in. Daimler's CD650 engine and Gardner's new 6LX (from 1958) were also offered in the long wheelbase chassis, these becoming the CVD650-30 and CVG6LX-30 respectively. The CVG6LX-30 was the most common long variant in British fleets.

A semi-automatic gearbox was introduced in 1957 which allowed gear changing without a clutch. This Daimatic transmission was offered as an alternative to the preselector gearbox, but with no change in the model designations. In the same year a restyled front end and bonnet assembly, designed to improve the driver's vision, was introduced. This was made of glassfibre and became known as the Manchester front, after the first customer to receive chassis fitted with it. Inconclusive experiments with turbocharged engines were also started in 1957.

In 1958, for the first time in over 25 years, a manual gearbox was made available in a Daimler bus chassis. The CSD6, CSG5 and CSG6 (S for

Below: *Rochdale Corporation bought 15 CVG6 with Weymann bodies in 1954 which were its last Daimler purchases for ten years. This picture shows one in its final Rochdale livery a few months before the undertaking and this bus were taken over by the Selnec PTE in November 1969.* / R. L. Wilson

Syncromesh) had a four-speed David Brown gearbox. Between 1959 and 1962 a mere 40 were delivered: five CSG5, eighteen CSG6 and seventeen CSG6-30. They were succeeded in 1963 by the CCG5 and CCG6 (C for Constant-mesh). These had Guy four-speed constant-mesh gearboxes; Guy and Daimler had both come under the common ownership of Jaguar in 1960-1. A total of 64 CCG6 and 33 CCG5 models was delivered by 1968 when production ceased. There were no 30ft long CCG models.

Another 1958 development was the export CVD650-220 single-deck chassis which had a 22ft wheelbase. It was joined by a Gardner-powered equivalent, the CVG6-220, which used the 10.45 litre 6LX engine or the 8.4 litre 6LW. Few were built.

The last Daimler-engined bus, a CVD6-30, was delivered in 1962 to Rossie Motors, Rossington leaving a choice of CVG5, CVG6, CCG5, CCG6, CVG6-30 and CVG6LX-30 front-engined chassis until the mid-1960s. The last CVG5 was in fact produced in 1960 (for Kowloon Motor Bus Company) but the CCG5 lasted until 1968 and was the last five-cylinder engined bus produced for operation in Britain. Burton-on-Trent received the final examples.

However, front-engined buses were considered unsuitable for one-man operation; they were thought to lack passenger appeal; and a Government grant, introduced in 1968, of twenty-five per cent towards the cost of a new bus was dependent on its being of an approved type. Front-engined buses were not included in the list of approved types and the last home market front-engined Daimlers were delivered to Northampton Corporation in October 1968.

The very last buyer of front-engined Daimlers was Hong Kong in 1971. These were 22ft wheelbase CVG6LW-34 models, a type introduced in 1967.

Below: *Burwell & District, which was a long-standing Daimler customer, purchased this D650HS with curvaceous Willowbrook coachwork in 1955. It had been an exhibit at the 1954 Commercial Motor Show.* / G. R. Mills

Left: *Typical of Swindon's buses is this 1956 CVG6 with well-proportioned Park Royal bodywork which still looked attractive when photographed in 1970. It carried 61 seated passengers.* / M. A. Penn

Below left: *Four D650HS models were used as the basis of 61-passenger standee buses by Swindon Corporation, which had problems with low bridges on a busy route. Park Royal built the 34-seat bodywork and the complete buses weighed over 7½ tons, which was more than many contemporary double-deckers. This bus was new in 1954.* / G. R. Mills

Above right: *Restrained Duple bodywork was specified by Cronshaw of London for this D650HS of 1955. When photographed in 1967 it was operating for Vines of Great Bromley.* / G. R. Mills

Right: *In 1956/57 Cardiff Corporation bought 15 CVG6 with East Lancashire Coachbuilders bodywork.* / D. G. Bowen

Left: *Halifax received its last front engined Daimlers in 1956. This is one of five Roe-bodied CVG6 and is shown at Todmorden in 1972. Halifax was involved in trials with turbocharged Daimler engines and also converted mid-1950s Daimlers to CVL6 specification with Leyland O.600 engines.* / M. A. Penn

Right: *Centre entrances for double deckers have never had widespread popularity and the six CVG6 delivered in 1956 to the Stalybridge, Hyde, Mossley and Dukinfield undertaking must surely have been the last of their type in Britain. The Northern Counties bodywork had 60 seats and a two-piece sliding door. These vehicles passed to the Selnec PTE and were not withdrawn until 1972. / Don Morris*

Below: *Marischal College provides a background for the last of a batch of 15 CVG6 models with Metro-Cammell Orion bodies delivered to Aberdeen Corporation in 1956. / Stewart J. Brown*

Above: *This was the first of Daimler's 30ft long two-axle double-deck chassis, introduced when the British Construction & Use Regulations were amended to permit operation of such vehicles. The chassis was exhibited at the 1956 Commercial Motor Show. Ultimately it was sold to Leon Motor Services, Finningley and it entered service in 1961 with a 73-seat Roe body and a Manchester style bonnet assembly. It was one of only two CVD650-30 models built, with Daimler's 10.6 litre engine.* / M. A. Penn

Right: *The second 30ft chassis was a CVG6-30 new in 1957, and fitted with 74-seat Willowbrook body. In 1958 a 10.45 litre Gardner 6LX engine was fitted in place of the 8.4 litre 6LW, this being the first bus to use the 6LX power unit. In 1961 it was purchased by McGill's Bus Service of Barrhead, for whom it was still running in 1977. It was one of only two 30ft long Daimler chassis to have a Birmingham style front.* / Stewart J. Brown

Above: *Western Australian Government Tramways purchased 20 D650HS with Howard Porter 45-seat bodywork in 1957/58. Some were later rebodied but this one, seen in the ownership of the Perth MTT in 1974, retained its original body.* / G. J. Travers

Above left: *Weymann Orion bodywork with its distinctive shallow upper deck windows was fitted to this Leeds City Transport CVG6. It was one of 20 similar vehicles delivered in 1957.* / M. A. Penn

Left: *Although Daimlers had been popular with independent operators in the early postwar period, very few were being purchased by small operators by 1957 when this CVG6 joined the Leeds based fleet of Samuel Ledgard. It had comparatively rare double-deck bodywork by Burlingham of Blackpool, now absorbed by Duple. This bus was acquired by the West Yorkshire Road Car Company in October 1967 when it took over the Ledgard company.* / G. R. Mills

Right: *The CVG5 was outwardly identical to its six-cylinder counterparts. The last home market CVG5 models were six with Roe 63-seat bodies supplied to Sunderland Corporation in 1958.* / Stewart J. Brown

Above: *This CVD6-30 with Northern Counties body was exhibited at the 1958 Commercial Motor Show. Its turbocharged Daimler CD6 8.6 litre engine was removed by Potteries Motor Traction in 1964 and replaced by a Leyland unit. It remained unique in the PMT fleet.* / Stewart J. Brown

Right: *In 1959 Leeds City Transport purchased 30 CVG6LX-30 with Roe bodywork. This one received a surprising new lease of life when it was purchased in 1975 by Dennis Motors and fitted with a Voith gearbox to monitor the compatability of the gearbox with Gardner's 6LX engine — this combination was being proposed by Dennis for its new rear engined Dominator bus chassis. The Daimler demonstrated on behalf of Dennis to a number of urban bus operators and is shown here in London in July 1977, newly repainted in London Transport red.* / Stewart J. Brown

Above: *Glasgow Corporation purchased 45 semi-automatic CVG6 and five CVD6 in 1959. The first buses to be delivered carried the traditional orange, cream and green livery shown here in this 1964 view of a CVG6; the later deliveries were in a simplified livery designed to facilitate spray painting. Alexander 61-seat bodies were fitted. These chassis had the original design of Manchester front featuring a narrow glassfibre front assembly with parallel sides.* / Stewart J. Brown

Centre left: *The more common version of the Manchester front tapered from bottom to top. This is one of only 18 CSG6 models built. Ten went to South Shields, six to Cardiff and two — one of which is shown here — to the Stalybridge, Hyde, Mossley and Dukinfield Joint Board. By 1959 the idea of separate top-sliding windows as fitted to the lower deck of this Northern Counties body was out of date.* / A. Moyes

Bottom left: *The CSG5 was a rare model — only five were made before it was superseded by the CCG5. Three CSG5s went to Burton and two to Grimsby-Cleethorpes. One of the latter, new in 1959 and with 63-seat Roe body, is seen passing Grimsby town hall in 1972.* / M. A. Penn

Above: *Burlingham Seagull bodywork is fitted to this Freeline coach of Blue Bus Services of Willington. It was a 1959 D650HS model.* / J. R. Neale

Right: *Cunningham's Bus Service of Paisley is one of the joint operators on the high-frequency service between Paisley and Renfrew Ferry. This 1959 CSG6-30 with Northern Counties 74-seat body was exhibited at the Scottish Motor Show. It was purchased by Garelochhead Coach Services in 1960 and is seen here in 1964 soon after it had been acquired by Cunningham.* / Stewart J. Brown

Below right: *Very few independents were buying new Daimlers in the late 1950s — a situation which the Fleetline was to change — and independently-owned CVG6 models with the Manchester-style bonnet were correspondingly rare. This 1960 example delivered to Blue Bus Services is also of interest in that it was the last Daimler chassis to be fitted with a side-gangway lowbridge body. It was bodied by Willowbrook.* / R. L. Wilson

Above: *Rather unfortunate front end styling marred the lines of the Northern Counties body fitted to this CVG6LX-30 of A1 Service from Ardrossan. It was purchased in 1960, at a time when members of the A1 co-operative usually bought second-hand buses.*
/ Alan Millar

Left: *The CCG6 replaced the CSG6 and had a constant-mesh gearbox. Ten were purchased by Chesterfield Corporation in 1963 and fitted with Weymann bodies to the Orion design, properly known as the Aurora when supplied with a forward entrance.*
/ M. A. Penn

Above: *In 1964 West Bromwich was buying Metro-Cammell bodied CVG6s and was still applying a delightfully complex paint scheme featuring two shades of blue and full lining out.* / T. W. Moore

Left: *South Shields Corporation was the best customer for the CCG6, buying 39 of the 64 built. This one is seen in the livery of the Tyne & Wear PTE on the last day of operation of open platform buses by the PTE, 24 April 1977. Volunteers manned the three last CCG6 on that day. Roe 63-seat bodywork was fitted to this 1964 bus.* / Tyne & Wear PTE

Above right: *The only operator to receive the CVG5 chassis with the Manchester style bonnet was the Kowloon Motor Bus Company in Hong Kong. This one was new in 1960 and has a Metal Sections body assembled locally from a kit of parts.* / Daimler

Right: *Burton Corporation favoured Gardner's 7 litre 5LW engine and Massey bodywork. Two 1964 CCG5 are shown here. In 1968 Burton purchased the last five-cylinder engined buses built — three CCG5 similar to those illustrated.* / T. W. Moore

Above: *The last Freeline built was this G6HS, one of three delivered in 1964 to Great Yarmouth Corporation. Roe built the 43 seat bodywork.* / G. R. Mills

Left: *Two batches of CVG6LX-30, totalling 55 in all, were delivered to City Tramways of Cape Town in 1965/66. They had fully-fronted bodywork by Bus Bodies (South Africa) and seated 79 passengers. The full front featured a Manchester grille flanked by brake cooling vents inspired by the Leyland PD3A St Helens style front.* / Stewart J. Brown

Above right: *A number of Yorkshire municipalities favoured big Daimlers. In 1966 Bradford bought 15 CVG6LX-30 with Neepsend 70-seat bodies. This one is seen in 1969 leaving Leeds for its home town.* / T. W. Moore

Right: *Swindon Corporation bought three CVG6-30 with 6LW engines and Northern Counties bodies in 1967. These were the last long front-engined Daimlers delivered to a British customer. The last one is illustrated in Thamesdown livery in 1977. Thamesdown had succeeded Swindon when local government was reorganised in 1974.* / G. R. Mills

Right: The last underfloor-engined Daimlers were 26 CVU6LX delivered to CCFL of Lisbon in 1967-68. These were in fact Guy Victory chassis with Gardner 6HLX engines and semi-automatic gearboxes. Six had UTIC 41-seat coach bodies as illustrated, while the balance had bus bodies, also by UTIC. / Daimler

Below: The end of an era. On 23 December 1971 the last of a long line of much respected front-engined Daimler bus chassis was driven out of the factory gates at Coventry. The last chassis, shown here, was a 21ft 6in wheelbase CVG6LX-34 and completed an order for 235 for the Kowloon Motor Bus Company, Hong Kong. / T. W. Moore

Front to Back

Daimler introduced its first rear-engined chassis in September 1960. This was the Fleetline RE30 with 16ft 3in wheelbase. The prototype had a Daimler CD6 engine but when production commenced the 10.45 litre Gardner 6LX was the standard engine (the 8.4 litre 6LW was an option chosen by few customers) and the type code was CRG6LX (R for **R**ear engined). The transmission and rear axle layout permitted a flat floor in the lower deck and the Fleetline could therefore be built as a low height (13ft 6in high) double-decker with a central gangway in each deck. This was a feature not then offered on Leyland's competing Atlantean model.

The Fleetline proved popular not only with traditional Daimler customers but with new ones too. It became the standard double-deck chassis for many companies in the British Electric Traction group and the Scottish Bus Group. London Transport purchased eight, for comparative trials with 50 Leyland Atlanteans, and ultimately ordered batches totalling 2,646 making LT the largest-ever Daimler fleet operator.

Below: One of the first Fleetlines to be bodied was this CRG6LW for A1 Service, the Ayrshire co-operative. It was exhibited at the 1961 Scottish Motor Show and has Northern Counties bodywork of a style fitted to most early Fleetlines bodied by that builder. This was the first Fleetline to have a 'shrouded' engine compartment which improved the profile of the rear of the bus by disguising the prominent engine installation. / M. A. Penn

In 1962 a 36ft long single-deck chassis was shown at the Earls Court Commerical Motor show. This had a horizontal Daimler CD6 engine mounted at the rear and was not intended as a production model. By the 1964 Earls Court show this chassis had been developed into the Roadliner with an 18ft 6in wheelbase and longitudinally rear-mounted Cummins V6-200 9.63 litre engine. Two years later the Perkins V8.510 (8.36 litre) was offered as an option. In this guise the Roadliner was known as the SRP8; with the Cummins engine it was the SRC6. It was the only British bus chassis at this time to be powered by a vee engine.

Most British-operated Roadliners were buses rather than coaches. Large overseas orders were received from Australia, Canada, and South Africa, and small numbers went to Europe — where some were sold as Guy Conquests. One Roadliner chassis formed the basis of a double-deck coach in Spain. The last Roadliners, built in 1972, were unique SRL8 models for Pretoria and were powered by the short-lived AEC-designed Leyland 810-series V8 engine of 13.1 litre capacity and 291bhp output. Ten 12-metre Roadliners were ordered by Johannesburg but were not built.

In 1967/8 a batch of 26 Daimler CVU6LX models was delivered to CCFL of Lisbon. This strange model was only a Guy Victory chassis with Daimler badges.

Although the 30ft long CRG6LX and CRG6LXB were by far the most common Fleetline models there were other variants. Walsall in 1962 received its first short Fleetline, only 25ft 7in long and with a 65-seat Northern Counties body. This was the forerunner of a fleet of short Fleetlines; similar vehicles were purchased by the Stalybridge, Hyde, Mossley and Dukinfield undertaking.

More common was the 18ft 6in wheelbase CRG6LX-33 and its SRG6LX-33 single-deck equivalent; these were designed for 33ft long bodywork, and the first entered service in 1967. In the following year the SRG6LX-36 was introduced for 36ft long single-deck bodywork. The availability of Fleetline chassis for single and double-deck bodywork allowed operators to standardise on one model for both uses, a practice which was of course common until the late 1940s. An SRG6LW was also available and used the smaller Gardner six-cylinder engine.

Below: *The first ever Fleetline was exhibited at the 1960 Commercial Motor Show and is shown here in service with Birmingham City Transport the following year. It had an 8.6 litre Daimler CD6 engine and was originally known as the RE30 model. It was later fitted with a Cummins engine and then with a Gardner 6LX. The body was by Weymann. / A. A. Cooper*

Vee-engines were tried experimentally in Fleetlines. A few had Cummins V6 engines — making them CRC6 — and one of Walsall's short models had a Perkins V8 thus becoming an unofficial CRP8. The vee engines were fitted transversely, unlike those in the fourteen CRC6/36 models built in 1968-69 which had 9.63 litre Cummins V6-200 engines mounted longitudinally in the rear offside corner of a 36ft long chassis designed for double-deck bodywork. All but one CRC6/36 (for Walsall) went to Johannesburg.

The merger in 1968 of British Motor Holdings (which controlled Daimler) and Leyland brought about some changes. In 1970 Leyland's 680 engine was offered in the Fleetline chassis as an alternative to the Gardner units, and this model was known as the CRL6. Then in 1973 the link between Daimler buses and Coventry was broken with the transfer of Fleetline chassis production (the only bus offered after the Roadliner's demise) to Leyland in Lancashire. The last Coventry-built Fleetline (7224 had been built) went to Hong Kong; the first Leyland-built Fleetline went to London Transport.

Leyland then dropped Daimler's established system of chassis designation. The 30ft CRG6LX became the FE30GR (**F**leetlin**E**, 30ft long, **G**ardner engine, **R**ight hand drive). The 33ft CRG6LX-33 became the FE33GR. Equivalent Leyland - engined models became FE30LR and FE33LR. A quiet Leyland engined version — bought by London Transport — was also known as the B20.

Rolls-Royce power has also been tried in Fleetlines. Five London Fleetlines have Rolls-Royce Eagle diesel engines and Cleveland Transit has experimented with liquified petroleum gas fuel in a Rolls-Royce-powered Fleetline.

In 1976 Leyland started referring to 'Leyland Fleetlines' — and from mid-1977 Leyland Fleetline badges replaced the Daimler name on new vehicles. Leyland's second-generation rear engined double-decker, the Titan TN15 announced in 1977, is intended to replace the Fleetline and other Leyland group double-deckers which will be phased out as demand for them falls.

Below: *In 1966 the original Fleetline, by that time a CRG6LX, was purchased by Blue Bus Services of Willington. Blue Bus was taken over by Derby Corporation in 1973. Sadly, this historic Daimler was one of 19 vehicles destroyed in a fire at the Willington depot in January 1976.* / T. W. Moore

Above: *The first big British Electric Traction group Fleetline order specified 50 CRG6LX with 77-seat Alexander bodies for the Midland Red fleet. These had flat glass in the windscreens on both decks in place of the curved glass normally used by Alexander. This bus, new in 1963, is seen at Meriden Hill. From this time Midland Red standardised on Alexander-bodied Fleetlines for its double-deck requirements; in the previous decade it had built all its own double-deckers.* / T. W. Moore

Right: *Warrington Corporation's first Daimlers were nine Fleetlines delivered in 1963. These had attractively proportioned 77-seat East Lancs bodywork. This one is seen at Bridge Foot, in central Warrington, in 1974.* / R. L. Wilson

Above: *Walsall Corporation was one of the few Fleetline operators to depart radically from the basic specification. This prototype short (25ft 7in) version had a 64-seat Northern Counties body with the entrance door behind the front axle. It was powered by a Gardner 6LX engine and was exhibited at the 1962 Commercial Motor Show. More followed (but were 27ft 6in long and 6LW powered) and later versions had doors immediately before and after the front axle. / T. W. Moore*

Centre right: *Only one batch of Fleetlines was purchased by Birkenhead Corporation. Nine CRG6LX with 77-seat Weymann bodies joined the fleet in 1964 when this one was photographed. An unusual feature for a front entrance bus was that the handles to change the destination screens were fitted outside the bus (above the nearside windscreen) rather than inside. / R. L. Wilson*

Bottom right: *Glasgow Corporation's last Daimler bus — it had purchased 362 since 1937 — was a solitary CRG6LX with Alexander body of an advanced style. It entered service in 1963, and cost £6,931 10s (£6,931.50). After running briefly for the Greater Glasgow PTE it joined the fleet of Graham's Bus Service, Paisley, in October 1975. It was not the only Fleetline to wear Glasgow Corporation colours. Demonstrator 565CRW was exhibited at the Scottish Motor Show in 1963 in full Glasgow livery — by strange coincidence it, too, was to join the Graham fleet. / Stewart J. Brown*

Above: *The Scottish Bus Group's first Fleetline was in fact ordered by Baxter's of Airdrie which was taken over by Scottish Omnibuses in 1962. It received the first lowheight Alexander body on a rear-engined chassis and was delivered to Scottish Omnibuses in 1963. It is seen here in Bathgate in 1964 en route from Glasgow to Edinburgh in its original light green livery; it was soon repainted in Baxter's blue.* / Stewart J. Brown

Centre left: *There was still some individuality in body design in the early 1960s, The Roe body on this 1964 Fleetline was of a style peculiar to Sunderland Corporation with peaked domes at the front and rear. It is waiting for passengers outside Binns — the shop most buses in the north east urge passengers to patronise.* / Stewart J. Brown

Below left: *Irish bodywork is rare in England and the only Irish-built double-deckers to run in the country are two Fleetlines with MH Coachworks bodies delivered to Bournemouth Corporation in 1964. MH bodied large numbers of Fleetlines for Belfast Corporation and also assembled the chassis which were shipped completely knocked down.* / M. A. Penn

Right: *Only one Fleetline received Massey bodywork. Even by 1964 standards this 74-seat lowheight body was uncompromisingly square — yet contemporary Massey bodies on front-engined chassis were still pleasantly styled. A member of the Ardrossan-based Ayrshire Bus Owners co-operative owned this unique bus, seen here reversing into the cramped and now abandoned A1 bus station in Kilmarnock. / Stewart J. Brown*

Below: *In 1965 London Transport bought eight Fleetlines for comparative trials with 50 Leyland Atlanteans. All had 72-seat Park Royal bodies and the Fleetlines were designed for use as one-man operated buses with the upper deck shut off by a door at the foot of the stairs. The Fleetlines were green country area buses — although they were also tried in the central area — and passed to the newly created London Country Bus Services on 1 January 1970. The last of the eight is shown here in April 1970 wearing a blue and silver livery used for the Blue Arrow service which operated in Stevenage and was a predecessor of the Superbus services. / G. R. Mills*

Right: *The idea of standardising on the Fleetline for single-deck as well as double-deck use was novel in 1965 when Birmingham took delivery of 24 Marshall-bodied CRG6LX. These buses seated 37. The first one is seen here in November 1965.* / T. W. Moore

Below: *The first export Fleetlines were 40 left-hand drive models for Portugal. The chassis were shipped completely knocked down and were assembled by UTIC. The 79-seat bodywork was built by the operator — CCFL of Lisbon. Rubbing strips are fitted to the roof to minimise damage from overhanging branches. These buses entered service in 1967/68.* / Daimler

Above: *West Bromwich Corporation was an old-established Daimler customer who stayed loyal to CVG variants until 1967 when a batch of Metro-Cammell-bodied CRG6LX was delivered. These buses featured a brighter livery and were of lowheight construction so that they could negotiate this bridge in Hyde Road.* / T. W. Moore

Right: *The main buyers of the lower-powered CRG6LW (of 8.4 litre capacity against the 6LX's 10.45 litre) were Middlesbrough and Grimsby-Cleethorpes. The latter bought 20 between 1965 and 1969 and the first one, with 70-seat Willowbrook body, is seen here in October 1965. From 1970 onwards the more common CRG6LX variant was purchased by Grimsby-Cleethorpes. Teesside Municipal Transport, as Middlesbrough's successor, turned to the CRL6 with Leyland 680 engine in 1971.* / R. L. Wilson

Below right: *Standardisation at Grimsby-Cleethorpes: 6LW powered single-deck Fleetlines were also uncommon but four — among the first SRG6LW to be built — joined the fleet in 1966/67. All had dual-door Willowbrook bodies.* / T. W. Moore

Left: *Twenty five Fleetlines formed the second batch of the type for Alexander's (Midland) and featured an experimental livery which was soon dropped. This bus, new in November 1967 illustrates that livery and the then new style of fleetname. / Stewart J. Brown*

Below left: *Ten 28ft 6in long Walsall-style Fleetlines were purchased in 1968 by the Stalybridge, Hyde, Mossley and Dukinfield undertaking and were its last new buses. They had 68-seat Northern Counties bodies with jacknife front doors and a sliding exit door immediately behind the front axle. The first of these 6LW engined buses is seen in Salford in July 1977 by which time it had passed into the ownership of Greater Manchester Transport. / M. A. Penn*

Right: *This 1968 CRG6LX, diverted from the Halifax fleet, is seen being loaded on the* Clan Maclean *for shipment to Cape Town where it demonstrated to City Tramways. It had a Northern Counties lowheight body; City Tramways subsequently purchased Fleetlines with locally-built bodywork. / Daimler*

Below: *The same bus in Cape Town in 1975. Deeper sliding windows have been fitted, and the curved windscreens replaced by flat glass, but the Northern Counties body outline is still recognisable. Behind is a Fleetline with bodywork by Bus Bodies (South Africa). / Stewart J. Brown*

Left: *Belfast Corporation was, according to Daimler in 1970, always noted for its advanced thinking on matters concerning passenger transport. The occasion for this comment was the introduction in February of that year of Belfast's first 36ft long Fleetline single-deckers. These were 30 SRG6LX-36 models with 43-seat Alexander (Belfast) bodies designed for one-man operation and a 20 year life. / Daimler*

Below: *Dundee Corporation had latterly standardised on Fleetlines, buying 105 double-deckers and 25 single-deckers between 1964 and 1975. All had Alexander bodies. The Dundee undertaking passed to Tayside Regional Council in May 1975. Two years later a 78-seat 1969 CRG6LX passes a 46-seat 1970 SRG6LX-33 in central Dundee. / Stewart J. Brown*

Above left: *With 86 seats, this CRC6-36 was one of the biggest double-deckers ever to run in Britain. It is shown here at the 1968 Commercial Motor Show prior to being delivered to Walsall Corporation. This bus had two doors — at the extreme front and rear — and two staircases. Closed circuit television with a screen behind the driver showed him what was happening on the rear platform. A Cummins V6 engine was fitted in the rear offside corner. Northern Counties built the bodywork on what was destined to be the only 36ft long urban double-deck bus in Britain. / T. W. Moore*

Left: *Sixteen production CRC6-36 models were delivered to Johannesburg Municipal Transport in 1969 and had Bus Bodies (South Africa) 85-seat bodies. They were later re-engined with General Motors V8 diesel engines. By 1975, when this one was photographed in Van der Bijl Square, they had been demoted to peak hour duties only. / Stewart J. Brown*

Above: *Since 1961 Barrow-in-Furness Corporation has purchased only single-deckers. Of these, five were SRG6LX-36 Fleetlines with unusually styled East Lancashire bodies featuring low windscreens and high side windows. Note the nearside destination screen. This bus was new in 1971 and is a 49-seater.* / J. R. Neale

Left: *At the start of the 1970s the Scottish Bus Group's standard double-decker was the Fleetline. This 1971 delivery to Scottish Omnibuses has an Eastern Coach Works body and is seen on test in central Edinburgh.* / Travel Press

Above right: *In 1971 City of Oxford Motor Services received 20 Fleetlines with 70-seat Alexander bodies. Unusually for lowheight buses these had two doors. This one is seen in central Oxford in February 1973 before the National Bus Company's corporate identity livery had become widespread.* / Stewart J. Brown

Right: *Eleven Northern Counties-bodied CRL6 were diverted from a Western Welsh order to London Country Bus Services which received them in January 1972. One is shown on a Sunday working to West Croydon bus station in 1976, still in original green and yellow livery.* / Stewart J. Brown

Left: *A minority of Scottish Bus Group Fleetlines has Northern Counties bodywork. This one is one of five originally intended for Western SMT which entered service with Alexander's (Fife) in December 1971 and passed to Alexander's (Midland) in 1975. It is shown leaving Glasgow's Buchanan Street bus station, closed in December 1976, en route for Cumbernauld new town. / Alan Millar*

Above right: *The Derby fleet contains five SRG6LX-33 with 43-seat Willowbrook bodies purchased in 1972. This February 1977 view shows one loading in Derby bus station on the ex-Blue Bus service to Burton. / T. W. Moore*

Right: *Johannesburg Municipal Transport built up a fleet of 33ft long Fleetlines in the mid-1970s. All are one-man-operated and have single-doorway Bus Bodies (South Africa) coachwork. Note the use of the Leyland name. / Stewart J. Brown*

Below: *Yorkshire Woollen District received its last Fleetlines in 1972. Twelve were delivered with full-height Eastern Coach Works 74-seat bodies. This photograph was taken at Dewsbury in the summer of 1973. / M. A. Penn*

SPEED LIMIT
6 M.P.H.

46

BURTON

ONE MAN OPERATED
Please tender exact fare

OCH 256L

Blossom
yellow margarine

587

LEYLAND
·12-366-886·

Right: *Graham's Bus Service of Paisley was one of the first Scottish independents to buy a Fleetline in 1963. In July 1976 two CRL6 versions with Alexander bodies were added to the fleet. One is seen here near Hawkhead in the summer of 1977.* / Stewart J. Brown

Below right: *The first rear engined double-deckers to be purchased by A. Mayne & Sons Ltd, the Manchester independent, were five CRG6LXB with 78-seat Roe bodies. They were new in 1976.* / J. R. Neale

Above: *The standard Cleveland Transit bus is the CRL6 with 70-seat two-door lowheight body by Northern Counties. By 1973, when this one was delivered, 76 were in service. The fleet number has an L prefix which indicates that the bus can operate under the 13ft 6in high bridge at Middlesbrough station.* / M. A. Penn

Right: *A Daimler for Leyland. Fishwick, the Leyland-based independent, owns this SRL6-36 with angular 48-seat Fowler (a Fishwick associate) bodywork seen pulling out of Preston bus station. It is one of five, two of which were delivered in 1973.* / Alan Millar

Below right: *The world's biggest Daimler user is London Transport, with 2,646 Fleetlines in service or on order. A Park Royal-bodied CRL6 is seen climbing to Old Coulsdon, one of the southern extremities of London Transport operation, in December 1976. It is crew operated.* / Stewart J. Brown

Above right: *Three Fleetlines with lowheight bodies joined the Derby fleet in March 1976 for use on ex-Blue Bus routes. These 78-seaters had glassfibre seats in the upper saloon. The appearance of the Alexander bodywork had changed little since the first examples were built in 1963.* / J. R. Neale

Right: *This 1970 CRG6LX-33 with 80-seat Park Royal body was diverted from the West Midlands PTE to Johannesburg Municipal Transport. It operated for a period in West Midlands livery but had received Johannesburg's maroon and cream livery when this photograph was taken in 1976.* / Stewart J. Brown

Below: *A more typical West Midlands Fleetline is this 1977 delivery with 76-seat Metro-Cammell body seen when new on a private hire in Coventry.* / Stewart J. Brown

Roadliner Roundup

Below: *There were high hopes for export Roadliners. In Canada, Edmonton Transit bought 28 and Calgary bought three — all with 44-seat Duple bodies whose heating system was designed to keep the driver's compartment warm enough to allow him to drive in normal clothing in sub-zero temperatures. A 1965 Edmonton SRC6 is illustrated.* / Daimler

Above right: *Home market buyers were few in number. Only one Roadliner was purchased new by a Scottish operator. Tumilty — one of the members of AA Motor Services — received this SRC6 with 52-seat Plaxton bus body in 1966. It was later fitted with a Perkins engine but is seen here approaching Irvine Cross when new — with its Cummins badge displayed on the front. / Stewart J. Brown*

Right: *Eastbourne Corporation purchased three SRC6 models with 45-seat East Lancs bodies in 1967/68. The first one is seen near the railway station in 1973. / M. A. Penn*

Below: *Twelve Roe-bodied SRC6 joined the Darlington fleet in 1967. All were two-door 47-seaters. An order for a further 12 was cancelled and single-deck Fleetlines purchased instead. / M. A. Penn*

Above right: *In Australia the Municipal Tramways Trust, Adelaide, bought 36 SRC6 chassis. One was a spare; the other 35 had 46-seat 8ft 6in wide bodywork by Freighter Industries. This, the first one, was three years old when photographed in 1972. An instruction on the bus stop reads 'One-man bus — enter at front' and the words 'Welcome aboard' are written alongside the entrance door. Note the location of the Daimler badge on the front. / N. Mackintosh*

Right: *A minority of Roadliners was used for coach duties. This smart looking Plaxton-bodied coach had joined the fleet of Progressive, Cambridge, when photographed in 1971. It was new to Black & White Motorways. / G. R. Mills*

Right: Photographed passing through Swindon when new in 1969, this was one of Black & White's penultimate batch of Roadliners. It had a 47-seat Plaxton body on an SRP8 chassis. Between 1966 and 1970 Black & White purchased 37 Roadliners; a further eight on order were cancelled.
/ T. W. Moore

Centre right: In 1968 Springs Municipal Transport, in South Africa, was one of a number of operators to purchase Roadliners in the model's biggest overseas market. This is one of four SRC6 with stylish Transvaal Motor Body Builders coachwork photographed in the bus station at Springs in 1975. / Stewart J. Brown

Below: Pretoria City Transport purchased 31 of the 61 Roadliners delivered to South Africa including the last chassis built in 1972. This SRL8 with 52-seat Transvaal Motor Body Builders coachwork is shown in Church Square, Pretoria's city centre terminal point. Note that it carries Leyland's name on the front, rather than Daimler's.
/ Stewart J. Brown

Trolleybuses

A small number of trolleybuses were built shortly before the outbreak of World War 1 and a few AEC trolleys were sold under the ADC banner in the late 1920s. The first modern Daimler trolleybus was built in 1936 and was followed by 24 more in 1937/38. The main pre-war customers were West Hartlepool and Derby. In the 1949-51 period a further 92 trolleybuses were delivered. Glasgow and Rotherham between them received 74 three-axle models while 18 two-axle models went to Pretoria, South Africa.

Trolleybus chassis designations began CT (**C**ommercial, **T**rolleybus) followed by a letter to indicate the make of electrical equipment fitted — C for **C**rompton Parkinson, E for **E**nglish Electric or M for **M**etrovick. The letters were followed by the figures 4 or 6 to indicate two- or three-axle chassis respectively.

Below: Daimler's first modern trolleybus chassis was this 1936 CTM4. It was bodied by Willowbrook and used as a demonstrator until 1938 when it was sold to South Shields Corporation. It is seen here after being rebodied by Roe in 1943. / Don Morris

Left: *West Hartlepool Corporation was the biggest prewar Daimler trolleybus customer, buying 14 CTM4 models with 54-seat Roe bodies with distinctive cab windscreen styling. This bus, which entered service in November 1938, was the last double-deck trolleybus purchased and was one of a small number owned jointly by West Hartlepool and neighbouring Hartlepool Corporation. It is seen outside the LNER Creosote Works in April 1952, twelve months before the trolleybus system closed. / Roy Marshall*

Below, left and right: *Rotherham Corporation purchased 44 single-deck Daimler trolleybuses in 1949/50. These CTC6s had 38-seat centre-entrance East Lancs bodies and were later exported to Cadiz, Spain. / R. L. Wilson, Daimler*

Right: *Twenty of Rotherham's single-deckers were given new Roe 70-seat double-deck bodies in 1956, including this CTE6. Six-bay bodywork was rare on vehicles of this period. Daimlers of this type were the last trolleybuses operated by Rotherham where the system closed in October 1965. / R. L. Wilson*

Above: *In 1938 Derby added six CTM4 models to its trolleybus fleet. They had 54-seat Brush bodies.* / Roy Marshall

Right: *Glasgow did not commence trolleybus operation until April 1949. In 1950 it received 30 CTM6 with London-style Metro-Cammell bodies seating 70 passengers. The last of these survived until 1964 and the Glasgow trolleybus system closed in May 1967. This picture taken in June 1950 shows a three-month old bus in its original livery.* / Roy Marshall

Birmingham Style

Below: *To speed deliveries in the early postwar period other operators were often prepared to accept a standard style of body, rather than wait for bodies built to their own specifications. Newcastle received 55-seat Birmingham style Metro-Cammell bodies on 14 CVG6 delivered in 1948.* / Roy Marshall

Right: *Birmingham Corporation's standard early postwar Metro-Cammell bodywork is illustrated by this 1948 CVG6 which still looked smart when photographed in 1962.* / G. R. Mills

Below: *Birmingham style bodies got as far north as Edinburgh. This CVG6 new in 1949 was one of 62, along with ten similar CVD6 buses.* / Harry Hay

Rebuilt and Rebodied

Below: *The COG5/40 had a compact engine installation to permit the fitting of high capacity (40 seat!) single-deck bodywork. This Trent example was delivered in 1938 with a Duple coach body but was rebodied as a 56-seat double-decker by Willowbrook in 1942. It survived in this form until 1953. / Roy Marshall*

Above: *Only 100 CWG5 were built. Lancaster had this 1943 chassis fitted with a Crossley body in 1952 to replace wartime Massey bodywork.* / M. A. Penn

Right: *The original Brush body on this 1945 CWA6 of Maidstone & District Motor Services was replaced in 1951 by the new Weymann body shown. It is seen in Maidstone in September 1964, shortly before its withdrawal, about to take up a peak trip on the Yeoman service.* / Stewart J. Brown

Below right: *Curvaceous 1953 lowbridge Massey bodywork is fitted to this Southend Corporation CWA6. It was new in 1944 with Duple bodywork and was one of 19 wartime Daimlers — some bought secondhand from London Transport — to be rebodied in the early 1950s. This bus, seen at Eastwood in December 1964, was withdrawn late in 1965.* / G. R. Mills

Right: *No, it's not a Leyland. Edinburgh Corporation had most of its wartime Daimlers rebodied by Alexander and fitted with Leyland style fronts. The full front body was an illusion: the nearside was not glazed. This bus, a 1944 CWA6, was rebodied in 1954 and at that time acquired a Gardner 5LW engine.* / Stewart J. Brown

Below: *The rebodying of a 17 year old chassis is extremely rare. This Daimler CH6 of Edinburgh Corporation was one of nine purchased in 1932 and fitted with Gardner 5LW diesel engines in 1934/35. Of these, six were rebodied by Alexander in 1949 and gave a further ten years' service. This one is seen in the early 1950s in the High Street.* / Don Morris

Left: *This CWA6 started life with London Transport in 1946. It was one of a batch of 100 with 56-seat Park Royal bodywork and is seen here after being sold to Belfast Corporation who later had it rebodied by Harkness.* / Don Morris

Right: *Cardiff's first postwar Daimlers were ten CVD6 which entered service between 1948 and 1950. All were fitted with East Lancashire bodies which were new in the 1944-46 period and had originally been fitted to 1932 Leyland Titan TD2 chassis for which they proved too heavy.* / Roy Marshall

Below right: *In 1957 the East Lancs bodies were removed and new 8ft wide Longwell Green bodies were fitted to the 7ft 6in wide CVD6 chassis. In this form the buses survived until the mid-1960s.* / D. G. Bowen

Below: *Belfast rebodied 100 ex-London CWA6 buses in 1955/56 and these are typified by this 1965 view of one with a 1956 Harkness 56-seat body.* / R. L. Wilson

Below: *Hartness of Penrith purchased a large number of new CVD6 chassis in the early postwar period to which were fitted secondhand bodies from a variety of sources. The bus on the left had an Eastern Counties 31-seat body of the mid-1930s which had previously been fitted to a North Western vehicle. That on the right had an Alexander body of a slightly later period. Both were later rebodied by Roe and Plaxton respectively. / R. C. Davis*

Right: *Very few wartime Daimlers were rebodied as single-deckers. One was this Newport CWA6 which started life in 1945 with a Park Royal 56-seat body and was rebodied in 1954 by D. J. Davies as a 32-seater. / Don Morris*

Bottom: *One of the buses illustrated above received this fully-fronted Roe 35-seat body in 1954, completely transforming its appearance. / G. Coxon*

Bottom right: *Few people would suspect that this 1955 Duple body was concealing a 1948 CVD6 chassis. The original body was by Yorkshire Yachtbuilders. Beehive of Ardwick-le-Street owned this coach. / G. R. Mills*

Above: *Aberdeen Corporation purchased seven CVD6 with locally built Walker single-deck bodywork in 1947/48. In 1958 two of these were rebodied by Alexander, receiving that builder's last half-cab single-deck bodies. When this photograph was taken in 1964 these vehicles were still in use on City Tours.* / Stewart J. Brown

Right: *Other Daimlers rebodied by Alexander for Aberdeen Corporation were ten CVG6 delivered in 1951 with 56-seat Northern Coachbuilders bodywork. In 1960 they received 66-seat Alexander bodywork of a style also supplied to Aberdeen on new CVG6 chassis from 1961 to 1965.* / Stewart J. Brown

Top left: *This 1962 CVG6 of Doncaster Corporation had a 1959 Roe body which was previously mounted on a 1945 trolleybus chassis. Doncaster treated 12 CVG6 chassis in this way. The thick pillar on the first bay of the upper deck carried electrical cables when the body was on a trolleybus.* / G. R. Mills

Centre left: *This Northern Counties-bodied CVG6 of AA Motor Services, Ayr, is not quite what it seems. It started life in 1950 as a CVD6 with a Plaxton coach body and was rebodied as a 63-seat forward-entrance double decker in 1962. Subsequently a Gardner 6LW engine was fitted and the centre portion of the bonnet assembly extended a few inches to accommodate it.* / Alan Millar

Below: *A rare rebodied Roadliner — indeed it may be unique. This SRC6 was supplied to Potteries Motor Traction with a Marshall body in 1967. The original body was destroyed by fire and a new Plaxton body fitted in 1969. But like most other Roadliners it was shortlived. Potteries sold it in 1975.* / M. A. Penn

Right: *The rebodying and rebuilding of buses became an operational hazard in Northern Ireland in the 1970s. This 33ft long CRG6LX, delivered in 1970 to Belfast Corporation, was one of two which in 1976 received Alexander (Belfast) bodies of a style usually fitted to Leyland Atlanteans. By that time Citybus had taken over the operation of Belfast's buses.* / R. C. Ludgate

Below: *Rebodied Fleetlines are not commonplace. Nottingham had some of its early examples fitted with new Northern Counties bodies using parts of the original bodywork which was also by Northern Counties. This example has a 1963 chassis and a 1975 body with distinctive Nottingham features such as an enclosed engine compartment and unusual frontal styling.* / J. R. Neale

Coventry Camera

Below: *This 1929 CF6 with 26-seat, two-door Brush body was Coventry Corporation Tramways' (as the undertaking was then known) first Daimler. It is seen in 1931 at the opening of Corporation Street. It was sold in 1935.* / T. W. Moore collection

Coventry, the home of Daimler, did not buy any Daimler buses for its municipal fleet until 1929 — when it purchased one. A second followed in 1933, AEC engined versions were tried in 1934, and from 1935 the COA6 was Coventry's standard double-decker. After the war CVA models were purchased, followed by CVD6, CVG6 and, from 1965, CRG6LX.

Right: *Typical of wartime deliveries is this 1944 CWA6, one of thirteen with 56-seat Northern Counties body. It is seen in Pool Meadow in 1958, looking very respectable for a 14 year old bus in its last year in service.* / T. W. Moore

Below right: *Roe bodywork was fitted in 1949 to this 1938 COA6 — it was one of five to be so treated. It was photographed in flood water at Spon Ends in 1955, three years before being sold.* / T. W. Moore

Above: *This 1938 Brush-bodied COA6 seated 55 passengers and weighed only 6¾ tons; its mainly cream livery was non-standard. Note the low mounted headlamps and the clear style of lettering used for the fleetname and numbers.* / Daimler

Right: *Coventry's COG5/60 models had the unusually high seating capacity of 60 for a 26ft long bus. This was achieved by using the Gardner 5LW engine, which was compact; minimum seat spacing; and fitting a rearward facing bench seat against the lower deck front bulkhead. To keep within weight limits these buses featured 12 volt instead of 24 volt electrics; single-skin panelling in places; reduced gauge handrails(!); and fewer half-drop windows. This example shown leaving Broadgate in ruined central Coventry in 1944 was new in 1940 and lasted till 1952. It had a Brush body with sliding panel in the roof. The bus in the background is a 1939 Metro-Cammell-bodied COA6.* / T. W. Moore collection

Left: Peacetime deliveries commenced a new fleet numbering series and bus number 1 entered service in 1948, It was a CVA6 with 60-seat Metro-Cammell body and is seen here being inspected by the Corporation's transport committee and the then general manager, Mr R. A. Fearnley (second from left). It was sold for scrap in 1966. / T. W. Moore collection

Below: In 1952 Coventry's first batch of Daimlers with Birmingham style tin fronts was delivered. These were 40 CVD6, some of which ran for 20 years. Metro-Cammell bodies of a style developed from bus 1 were fitted; all subsequent front engined Daimlers had Metro-Cammell Orion type bodies. / A. A. Cooper

Above: *To many enthusiasts the typical Coventry bus is the CVG6 with Metro-Cammell Orion body and Manchester style front. Between 1958 and 1963, 122 were purchased. This one was new in 1959 and joined the West Midlands PTE fleet when it absorbed Coventry in 1974.* / A. A. Cooper

Right: *In 1959 three 41-seat Willowbrook-bodied Freeline coaches were purchased. They had Daimler engines. The first one is seen passing Coventry Cathedral in 1962. All were sold in 1970.* / T. W. Moore

Right: *The first Fleetlines also had Willowbrook bodies. This is one of 22 purchased in 1965 — along with a batch of Leyland Atlanteans which caused some consternation locally. The rural setting is Cropredy, near Banbury, venue of a private hire.* / T. W. Moore

Below: *Subsequent Fleetlines commenced yet another new series of numbers from 1 in 1966 — and had reached 142 by 1973. Bodies by Willowbrook, East Lancs and Eastern Coach Works are seen here; one other batch had Park Royal bodies. This 1969 view of Broadgate also shows four CVG6.* / T. W. Moore

Northampton Narrative

Northampton Corporation was for many years a loyal Daimler customer: at times its fleet has been a hundred per cent Daimler. The last of its CVG6 is expected to survive till the early 1980s, which will make Northampton one of the last operators of rear platform buses in Britain.

Below: A 1946 CWA6 with Duple 56-seat highbridge body. / Don Morris

Above: *Roe bodies were usually favoured, but this is one of 20 Northern Coachbuilders-bodied CVG6s purchased in 1947. It was photographed in 1964 in the centre of the town.* / T. W. Moore

Above right: *Two generations of Roe-bodied Daimlers leave St James depot for lunch time peak specials in June 1959. On the right is a 1939 COG5, on the left a 1953 CVG6.* / T. W. Moore

Right: *The last front-engined Daimlers to enter service in Britain were five CVG6 purchased in 1968. They had a few other 'lasts' to their credit. They were the last open-platform double-deckers built in Britain; the last pre-selector gearbox buses; and they had the last traditional Roe teak framed composite bodies. This one was photographed in November 1968, soon after entering service.* / T. W. Moore

Below: *After the CVG6, Northampton turned to single-deck Fleetlines with 45-seat two-door Willowbrook bodies designed for one-man-operation. Surprisingly these were SRL6-36 models, introducing* *Leyland 680 engines to an almost entirely Gardner powered fleet. Twenty joined the fleet in 1973.* / T. W. Moore

Manchester Miscellany

Below: One of the large COG5 fleet with streamlined English Electric bodywork purchased in 1940/41. This bus lasted until 1959 when it was withdrawn and sold for scrap. It is seen in Piccadilly in 1955. / R. L. Wilson

Manchester Corporation bought Daimlers and ADCs in the 1920s. Apart from one CH6, no further Daimlers were purchased until 1940 when 73 COG5s were added to the fleet; over 100 were on order but some chassis were destroyed in an air raid on Coventry. In the postwar years CWA6, CVG6, CCG6, CRG6LX and CRG6LXB models were purchased.

Above: *Brush bodies to a Manchester/Crossley design were fitted to 50 CVG5 delivered in 1947/48. The last were withdrawn in 1968. / Don Morris*

Top right: *Between 1953 and 1955 90 Metro-Cammell-bodied CVG6 joined the fleet. This was the oldest batch of vehicles to pass intact to the Selnec Passenger Transport Executive on its formation in 1969. / Don Morris*

Right: *A new style of bonnet assembly, moulded in glassfibre, first appeared on a batch of 30 CVG6 models delivered to Manchester in 1957 and soon became the standard design on Daimler chassis. The Burlingham bodywork on these buses seated 65. This photograph was taken in March 1958 when Manchester's Piccadilly bus station was being reconstructed. / R. L. Wilson*

Above: *Manchester Corporation bought its first Fleetlines in 1962. In 1968 the first to have a new style of body with square lines and deep windscreens — the Mancunian — were delivered. This Mancunian had a 96 passenger (75 seat) Park Royal body on a 33ft long CRG6LXB chassis. Although in Manchester red and white livery this bus was delivered new to the Selnec PTE in 1970 and was photographed in March of that year.* / R. L. Wilson

Right: *Selnec developed the Mancunian body style into its own standard design. This 1977 CRG6LXB of Greater Manchester Transport has a Northern Counties 75 seat body and is one of 350 broadly similar buses, some of which are bodied by Park Royal.* / R. L. Wilson

Below: *This Northern Coachbuilders-bodied COG5 of 1939 is seen running for the Llandudno & Colwyn Bay Electric Railway in July 1957. It was new to Newcastle Corporation. The Llandudno & Colwyn Bay was the last company-owned street tramway in Britain when it ceased tramcar operation in March 1956. The replacement bus service was taken over by Crosville in May 1961. / R. L. Wilson*

Topless Daimlers

Above: *Park Royal bodywork, converted to open top in 1956, was fitted to this 1945 CWA6 which joined the Southend municipal fleet in 1955. It was new to Birmingham City Transport and reached Southend via Benfleet & District and Westcliff-on-Sea Motor Services. It lasted until 1970.* / M. A. Penn

Right: *Convertible Weymann bodywork — the top cover can be fitted for winter use — is fitted to this 'county class' CRG6LX of Bournemouth Corporation. 'Yorkshire' is a 74-seater new in 1966 and one of a batch of ten. Seven of these buses were sold to London Transport in 1977 for use on its Round London Sightseeing Tour.* / R. L. Wilson